40 Tips on
Creative Writing

A GUIDE FOR WRITERS TO TURN YOUR
PASSION INTO A SUCCESSFUL BOOK

Dan Buri

DJF
Portland, Oreg

D1428051

Published by DJB Publishing

Book Layout ©2017 BookDesignTemplates.com
Book cover design and layout by, Ellie Bockert Augsburger of Creative Digital Studios.
www.CreativeDigitalStudios.com
Cover design features: Workplace writer. Flat design. © theromb / Adobe Stock

Ordering Information:
Quantity sales. Special discounts are available on quantity purchases by corporations, associations, and others. For details, contact the "Special Sales Department" at the address above.

40 Tips on Creative Writing / Dan Buri. —2nd ed.

For the writer in all of us.

And for my beautiful children, Isla and William.

Introduction

The life of an author can be difficult. As writers, we simply love to write. Unfortunately, getting our work published is never as simple as just writing. Often times we can't sit down and write because there are too many other tasks required of us. Publishing in the current environment of the internet, online publications, and ebooks is almost as simple as a click of button, but writing and publishing successfully is far more daunting. There are thousands of decisions to be made.

First you must decide what you want to write. Then you must sit down and write it. Is your idea best suited for a novel? A short story? An essay? A poem? And that's the part we love as writers—the actual writing. Then there's deciding on publishers, editors, agents, cover design, distribution channels, marketing, and on and on. Having struggled for years on the path to getting published, I know how difficult it can be.

I wrote this book in hopes of making it a little easier for you. Whether you're just starting out or you're starting out again, I aim to be your advocate on this writing journey. I started my website _www.Nothinganygood.com_ to support authors and writers as they navigate the difficult path to publication. Many of my readers asked for this book to be written. These 40 Tips are here because you asked for it, friends, and I'm grateful you did! I want to share what I've learned and be a voice of encouragement along this winding road of writing.

What do I have to offer? Well, I've been there, deep in the ups and downs of being a writer. I published my first fiction work, _Pieces Like Pottery_, a few years back. My non-fiction works have been distributed online and in print for nearly a decade now. I know the painstaking difficulty of trying to get published. I have suffered the demoralizing experience of wanting readers and finding none. And I kept writing anyway.

My website's namesake is an homage to the most famous writer from my home state of Minnesota, F. Scott Fitzgerald, "Nothing any good isn't hard." As in, anything good in life that you create is hard to create. Writing is hard. If you've written and been published before, you know this. If you're dreaming to become published, you have a mountain to climb and you should understand that before you begin. Please don't shy away. If your book is good, it should be hard to write. Most things in life worth doing are hard.

If you read _Pieces Like Pottery_, you may recall one of the lead characters found a list of Forty Tips for College and Life from his former high school teacher, Mr. Smith. I've received a lot of positive feedback on these forty life tips. They resonated deeply for readers. I've adapted the 40 tips for the sole purpose of helping you to become a published writer. One step at a time.

Like anything in life that's difficult, the best way to approach it is to break it into pieces. Figure out how to tackle your writing problems in steps. Break it down into actionable pieces that you can accomplish. Soon, as you complete one step after another, you will see your writing in print in no time. While you read through this book, if you're reading the print version, there is a Notes section at the end of the book. If an idea comes to you as you're reading, write it down. (Always write down your ideas!)

Thank you for joining me on this journey. We are on it together! May these tips bring you that much closer to realizing your dreams as an author.

Dan Buri is a trusted resource for writers to gain insight into the difficult world of indie publishing. His first collection of short fiction—Pieces Like Pottery—which has been recognized on multiple Best Seller Lists, is an exploration of heartbreak and redemption. His nonfiction works have been distributed online and in print, in publications including Pundit Press, Tree, Summit Avenue Review, American Discovery, and TC Huddle. Dan is a founding member of the Independent Writers Guild, a worldwide organization of writers and publishing professionals dedicated to promoting the interest of indie writers by encouraging public interest in, and fostering an appreciation of, quality indie literature. He is an active attorney in the Pacific Northwest. He lives in Oregon with his wife and two young children.

Life is too short not to seize the opportunities presented to us. Always take the chance to do what you love when it comes along.

D o you lie awake dreaming of writing a book? Have you written a book before and now you're thinking about writing your next one? Do interesting stories pop into your head throughout the day? Do you see events play out before you on the street and immediately think it might make a good story? Do you find yourself thinking about writing, but don't actually sit down to do it?

Start writing. You only need thirty minutes a day. Life's too short to not write if that's what you love to do. That first step is simple: Sit down and write.

I vividly remember when I first started to consider writing as more than a hobby fifteen years ago. Before then, I had an unfortunate mantra: "I'll write when…" As in, "I'll write that story when I have a long uninterrupted weekend." Or, "I'll write that book when my job isn't so busy." It was a mantra that was crushing any hope of taking my dreams of being a writer and actually becoming serious about writing. I realized there was never going to be a perfect time to write, so I threw that mantra out the window for good.

If I hadn't, I wouldn't have found myself writing for a number of print and online publications. I would have never started four different blogs over the last fifteen years, something that has been critical for me in learning how to hone my skills as a writer. I would have never become a published non-fiction writer and the author of an Amazon bestselling book of literary fiction. Now I have a new mantra: "I'll write now."

Whether you're writing your first book or your tenth, sit down today and write. Block off thirty minutes today.

Write that book!

Do you have thirty minutes today? Sit down and start writing now.

Don't be afraid to see dinosaurs even when no one else does.

This tip is one part Noah and the Great Flood and two parts The Emperor's New Clothes. I know, I shouldn't be this excited about my own writing tip, but what else have we got if we can't be excited about our own writing? It applies to many aspects of our writing journey, but there is one aspect in particular that I'd like to magnify.

Anyone who has ever tried to write something of worth, and any creative-type who has ever tried to make something out of nothing, knows how simultaneously exciting and scary it is. You have the archetypal blank canvas in front of you and can create whatever you want. The power rests in your hands.

I'm here to say go for it. Take all of that excitement and fear, and utilize it.

Don't worry about how others say you're supposed to write. Write the way you want to write. Sure, soak in all the advice and feedback from the writing experts and writing amateurs alike. Take it all to heart. Let it wash over you. Then filter it through that beautiful brain of yours and write the way you feel called to write.

You do you. You have a unique gift simply by having the desire to write a story. That's wonderful! Don't be afraid to see the world as you want to see it. You're the author. You get to create the reality of the characters. You get to define the scope of your essay. You're the architect of the memoir you're writing. Don't be afraid to see dinosaurs. J.K. Rowling saw dinosaurs. C.S. Lewis saw dinosaurs. Abraham Lincoln saw dinosaurs. Dostoyevsky. Dickens. Shakespeare. Aeschylus. They all saw dinosaurs. Don't be afraid to see your own dinosaurs.

Shakespeare

Charles Dickens

C.S. Lewis

J.K. Rowling

They all saw dinosaurs. Don't be afraid to see your own.

Be conscious of the present. Time is your most valuable asset.

You may be incredibly smart. You may have the wit of a thousand comedians. Your command of the English language may be beyond comparison, creating new words by the dozens like Shakespeare did. Being smart or witty or a wordsmith are all wonderful traits to have as a writer, but none of them compare to something that is common to us all—_Time_.

As a quick aside, I'm always amazed at how many words we use today that Shakespeare made up. I find it staggering. He has been credited with inventing over 1700 words that we currently use in the English language. 1700?!?

Here are some of my favorites:

Moonbeam (A Midsummer Night's Dream)

Cold-blooded (King John)

Bedazzled (Taming of the Shrew)

New-fangled (Love's Labour's Lost)

Puking (As You Like It)

Scuffle (Antony and Cleopatra)

Fashionable (Troilus and Cressida)

Swagger (Henry V)

Assassination (Macbeth)

Eyeball (The Tempest)

Addiction (Othello)

Laughable (The Merchant of Venice)

Inaudible (All's Well That Ends Well)

Uncomfortable (Romeo and Juliet)

Zany (Love's Labour's Lost)

Dishearten (Henry V)

Back to the point at hand. _Time._

Think about it for a moment. There are many things that can make you a renowned and successful writer, but every successful writer has one thing in common with each other. They all dedicated time to sit down and write.

Time is by far our greatest asset. Time abounds. You have more time than you realize. Even if you have a full-time job and are raising a family, you still have time. If I can do it, you can too!

Some writers wait for the moment of inspiration to strike. These moments are amazing, but they are a luxury. To begin taking your writing to the next level, to learn to hone it as a craft rather than viewing it simply as an inspirational hobby, start writing regardless of whether the circumstances are perfect.

Maximize the little blocks of time throughout your day to start writing.

Years ago, when I was in high school, I played four sports. (Yes, many, many years ago.) Whenever I was in between a sports season and without practice, workouts, and games, my grades weren't as strong. I realized that when I was busy, I had to optimize every thirty minutes I had to do my coursework, so I'd often do a half hour before or between classes. I'd also take time before dinner to complete assignments.

When I wasn't in-season, there was always time to do it later. What happened was that the time I had to do it later quickly vanished. When I was less busy, I procrastinated more.

Learn to maximize those little bits of time throughout the day. I'm not saying you have to go-go-go every second. That's not healthy. You need time to relax and rest. But I guarantee you can find at least a spare twenty to thirty minutes every day to write.

Is it in the morning before everyone is awake? Is it the later hours of night before you lay down? Is it on your lunch hour? Is it on your drive to work and you want to dictate your writing?

Start small. Find a little block of time each day where you are usually mindlessly putzing around and use that time to write. Try it on for size. I bet after a month, you'll be shocked at how much writing you've accomplished in just that short block of time.

Don't dress like a bum all day long.

You may disagree with me on this, which is fine. Some people do perfectly well rolling out of bed and doing great things in their underwear all day. I'm not one of those people. If I want to be productive, I prepare for it. Production doesn't just happen magically.

Wake up early. Shower. Wear respectable clothes. Eat breakfast. Get your mind right for writing. Then, when you're good and ready, sit down and write. Don't expect brilliant words to flow out of you as you sit in your pizza-stained sweats with a hole in the crotch.

When I started writing, I thought it needed to be in a particular time and place. I would typically write at night and would need to be in the perfect mood to do so. With a very demanding job, a wife, and two young kids, I realized that I was not finding time to write at all. I had to begin writing anytime I had a free thirty minutes.

I was lucky I did. Having such a limited timeframe to write each day helped me begin taking my writing to the next level. I began to view writing as a serious endeavor I wanted to learn and master. I had to find the time whenever I could, regardless of whether the circumstances were perfect. (That being said, I still love to write at night over a glass of wine or a Scotch. Nothing beats that.)

Truth is, the more I learn about the craft of writing, the more I realize that much of what we write when surged with inspiration ends up getting cut from the final print anyway. It's not for lack of good intentions. There just seems to be a disconnect between what we're picturing in our mind's eye and what we're putting down on paper when we're over excited with that inspiration. You'll find that some of your best writing will come out of you during those scheduled times when you're just not feeling it at all.

> **If you struggle to find time to write, schedule it. It's part of being a diligent writer.**

It may sound boring to have scheduled writing times, but it is incredibly important if you're looking to continue to refine your craft. It will keep you from deciding to watch TV or clicking on that cat video on YouTube. If you've scheduled it in, you'll be more prone to actually write during that time. Even if all you do is sit there staring at the page, hands frozen over the keyboard, it's valuable time spent. Don't get up to do something else. Don't worry about the lack of productivity. Just hold that space for writing even if half the time you're not even moving your fingers. It will produce good writing habits from which you'll reap the benefits.

Foster habits of a successful writer.

I f you want to write, start fostering the habits of a successful writer. Get rid of the ineffective patterns that prevent you from exploring your craft the way you want to. Turn off your screens from time to time.

This may be obvious to some of you, but it's probably counterintuitive to others. After all, how are you supposed to finish writing that great novel if you aren't disciplined enough to sit down at your laptop and write? But I firmly believe this is an absolute must. If you don't turn off your screens, you won't be the best writer you can be. We all struggle to find time in the day to do all the things we need to do. We have to be diligent. Don't waste time in front of screens you're not writing on.

You have very limited time that you can dedicate to your writing each day.

Do yourself a favor, be a serious writer. Don't waste time online.

I know that keeping up with emails and social media is necessary, especially for us indie authors. This is our avenue for creating a community around our books. Without it, the few sales we do get, quickly turn into that one copy that your family bought.

But how often do you check your email? How many times do you flip through your Twitter feed or Facebook updates? Did you really need to know that Linda's dog ate a cookie today? I don't know Linda or her dog, but I'm guessing it's not that interesting. Most of us can safely remove a dozen times we absent-mindedly check email and social media every day, at least. I know I can. Remove that mindless urge to check now!

After you've taken out some of the senseless internet scrolling, think long and hard about the blogs you visit. (I'm obviously not talking about www.*Nothinganygood.com*. That little website I've created to help support authors is a necessary part of your day, right!?) How many of those blogs that you read are nonsense reads that feed the beast of time-wasting?

In 2012, Digital Buzz put out an Infographic depicting the number of new blogs that are posted every day—two million. Two Million blog posts were going up every day back in 2012! Every. Single. Day.

Daily blog posts have more than doubled since then. We waste far too much time skimming blogs that we don't even really want to read. Was it necessary to learn about the 5 Celebrities That Secretly Wish They Were Authors? (*Number 3 will shock you!*) Stop wasting your time on them. Focus on the posts that will inform your writing, not the ones that will distract you from it.

Finally, turn off the TV! Stop watching YouTube! Shut down Netflix!

I love television and movies as much as the next person. I'm not here to tell you that TV is trash and you're rotting your brain. You're not. Television can be fantastic. Movies are wonderful. But stop watching so much. Spend more time exploring and developing your writing skills.

Successful writers foster effective writing habits. The most ineffective habit of an author is failing to write. The second is failing to budget time. If you can't manage thirty minutes a day to start, schedule in at least a couple blocks of time each week for writing, and when you sit down for that scheduled time, actually write. Don't waste it on other things.

Don't close your laptop just to pick up your phone.

Don't shut off your phone just to turn on the TV.

There's budgeting the time to write and then there's actually writing. All too often we sit down to write and we don't utilize that time for writing. We fiddle with previous chapters we've written. We spend far too much time trying to write that perfect sentence. We hop on the internet to do research for our writing. There will be time for all of that, either while doing research or later on in the editing process. Your writing time is for writing. If you've set that time aside, then write. The first draft is never good. Don't worry about it. Keep writing.

Cultivate the habits of successful writers if you want to become a better writer. Turn off your screens and begin the muscle-building of becoming the writer you want to be.

There is only one you.

T his tip is simple and intricately complex all at once. It's easy to understand, but can be a challenge to execute.

When you write, be you. Be as authentically you as only you can be. Don't try and emulate the voice of another writer. Write your own story in your own voice. Write what you're passionate about and write what you know. If you don't, the reader will see right through you and feel the disingenuousness in your writing.

My first work of fiction was a collection of linked short stories that are thematically modeled off of the Sorrowful Mysteries from the Catholic tradition of the Rosary. Say what? Snooze fest, right? I know. That's not going to sell at all! No one will ever want to read that.

Yet here I am. I reached #1 bestseller on a number of Amazon's book lists. My book was recommended by *The San*

Francisco Globe: "A story for everyone. It hits you in the feels."

Write what you're passionate about. If you don't, the reader will see right through you.

I recognize that there is some luck in this success. I don't deny that for a moment. But I do know that my book would not have come close to reaching the level of success it did, had I not written it with passion. My passion. In my own voice. I wrote what called to me regardless of whether or not it would see commercial success. Hell, I honestly didn't know if the book would even reach the light of day!

It took me seven years to write it and I had more than my fair share of doubts throughout its journey. Despite those doubts, I had to write what was welling up inside of me. I owed that to myself and to my readers. Anyone who writes anything with passion and authenticity is more likely to captivate their audience, no matter how big or small that audience is.

When my godson turned two, I bought him a piggy bank train. (A trainy bank?) On the bottom, I had the following Dr. Seuss quote inscribed:

"Today you are you, that is truer than true. There is no one alive who is youer than you."

- Dr. Seuss

I love this quote. It's beautiful.

All anyone can ever ask of us each day is to be the best possible version of yourself. That's it. That's all they can ask. And it's all we can, and must ask of ourselves.

The same goes for writing. Create the best version of yourself in every line you write. In your voice, with your unique experiences and imagination. Your rhythm, your mannerisms, your way with words, your story. No one else's.

There is only one you. Only one person can write what you're meant to write. Remember this every time you take the pen to the page, or place your fingers to the keyboard.

Dance in the rain.

I f you don't want to do this because it might make you a better writer, then do it because it's fun. When was the last time you danced in the rain? It's delightfully invigoration.

When my wife and I were dating years ago in college, we came home from a date one night and it was pouring rain. It was one of those nights where the rain comes down in sheets. Before going inside, we turned the music up on the car speakers and danced in the thunderstorm. To this day, I have no idea why we did this or how it came about, but it was liberating.

We stood in the middle of the street and danced our hearts out. My wife even climbed onto the hood of the car and danced right on top of it.

Granted, we shared some wine during dinner and that may have helped us "be free," but I look back on that moment as one of my favorite memories of our young love. Has it made me a better writer? I like to think so. It's this type of whimsical spontaneity that frees us from the doubts that prevent us from writing what we feel truly called to write. We need to be free to write without inhibition.

Find your voice as a writer and don't let go of it. Write the Real You.

Writing what is real for you is the heart of the matter. We often cling to how we think things should be. We're worried about writing a sketchy scene in our novel, or concerned what our family will think when writing our personal essays. We can't seem to let go of our uncertainties. Dancing in the rain is a metaphor for letting go. Let go of the fears, shame and resistance. Just write what your heart is yearning to write.

In Mary Karr's *The Art of Memoir* she says:

> *"During my short college stint, every time I picked up a pen, this grinding, unnamed fear overcame me—later identified as fear that my real self would spill out. One can't mount a stripper pole wearing a metal diving suit. What I needed to write kept simmering up while I wrote down everything but that. In fact, I kept ginning out reasons that writing reality was impossible. I cranked up therapy and drank like a fish."*

And then:

> *"Real You is all you have, and all other paths are false. And in the best case, Real You is so happy to finally be recognized, it rewards you with Originality."*

Whether you're writing fiction, non-fiction, historical romance, memoir, or children's books, be the Real You. Don't hesitate. Dance in the rain. Don't let the expectations of others muzzle the Real You.

Have a routine, but avoid being routine.

H aving a routine is good. We previously agreed in Tip 4 not to dress like a bum all day. This is part of planning to be productive. Having a routine and a schedule can ensure that you are actually writing, not just thinking about writing.

But don't let that routine control you. Follow it as far as it leads on the road of utility, but the moment you hit a dead-end and it's no longer useful, break away from it. Having a daily routine is valuable when it's helping your writing productivity, but there are times you need to change that routine entirely to get the creative sparks flying again.

Avoid being routine.

The creator and long-time producer of Saturday Night Live, Lorne Michaels, was once asked why SNL still uses the same weekly planning format that they have used since the 1970s. In light of today's technology, why were three long brainstorming nights still necessary?

His response? He said he wanted his team to be tired. When people are tired, they put their guard down. They forget about social norms and what is expected of them. Sure, a lot of lines are crossed in the brainstorming process, but the truly great comedy sketches also come directly from when his team is no longer worrying about what anyone thinks of them. Michaels believes that having the structure of a routine is valuable. That's why he hasn't changed it since the 70s. He also understands the value of breaking the routine. That's why despite a weekly format, he requires the team to work into the wee hours when how to think and how to write, and what his team thinks is funny, gets distorted. Through a weekly routine, he forces them into a position where they are tired and fall out of their habitual mode. He pushes them outside of their comfort zone to generate unique creativity.

Push yourself outside of your comfort zone. This is when the most creative moments happen. Avoid being routine. It will help your writing flourish.

Avoid being routine as a writer. Go outside your comfort zone.

My parents came to town recently for a visit. We were having friends and family over for Easter brunch and had to move the furniture around to accommodate an open floorplan for guests. After our friends left that day, I looked around the room and said, "I'm not sure whether I like this new set up or not." To which my mother remarked, "I think it works well, and you can always just move the furniture back."

She is a brilliant woman, my mother. I *could* always just move the furniture back if it turns out I don't like the layout.

My mind wandered away from moving furniture to other times in life when I'm too often afraid to try something new. This is particularly true in my writing. I'm not sure why I let the fear paralyze me, especially when I can always try out a writing project and drop it if it's not working. I can ditch a plotline in my book if it doesn't turn out the way I imagined.

Taking risks is crucial as a writer. Go ahead, dip your toe in the water.

As writers, we are often afraid of going outside our comfort zone. We are reluctant to move that furniture around. I'm here to tell you, as someone who is constantly plagued with fear and doubt, taking risks is crucial as a writer. Go ahead. Dip your toe in the water. I'll bet you'll find that it's not that bad and soon enough, you'll be wanting to dip your entire foot in. Or maybe even your whole body!

I am reminded of the famous Teddy Roosevelt quote:

> "The credit belongs to the man who is actually in the arena, whose face is marred by dust and sweat and blood; who strives valiantly; who errs, who comes short again and again, because there is no effort without error and shortcoming...who at the best knows in the end the triumph of high achievement, and who at the worst, if he fails, at least fails while daring greatly, so that his place

shall never be with those cold and timid souls who neither know victory nor defeat."

It takes courage to be vulnerable and create something, whether it's a book, art, a company, a family, or anything in life. It takes immeasurable courage to Dare Greatly. As a writer, you will take many courageous risks which are essential and commendable.

Whether you are wondering if you should risk trying something new with your writing or if you should try your hand at writing altogether, go ahead and do it. It doesn't matter what anyone thinks. What matters is what YOU think. And how you feel.

Rearrange the furniture, my friend. You can always move it back.

We are all intelligent, thoughtful individuals. Don't let others tell you something has to be *that way*. It doesn't. The world is far too complex to have it be *that way*.

I recently posted this tip on twitter. I received the following response from a follower: "no,they´re not. half of em is stupid and the half of that is even more stupid" (Note: my editor tried to put in [sic] and quickly found she was putting [sic] in every other word. Welcome to Twitter-speak friends!)

Anyway, even if I take this gentleman's flippant claim at face value, which I don't, he's claiming that 25% of the population is not stupid. That's a lot of people that aren't stupid! That's 80 million people in the U.S.; 16 million in the U.K.; 6 million in Australia and 1.8 billion people in the world!

Sorry internet troll, despite your negative attitude and even if I take your premise at face value, it's still enough people for me to take Creative Writing Tip 9 seriously.

So, what does this tip mean for us as writers? Everything! Apply this to every part of your writing life! Things don't have to be *that way*. Try something new in your writing.

The hottest thing on Broadway over the last two years was *Hamilton*. The hip-hop musical about Alexander Hamilton has now begun its national tour. I'm sure it will continue to draw massive crowds for years. That's ridiculous, right? Yep, and it's been the most difficult ticket to get for over two years. It was nominated for a record-setting sixteen Tony Awards, winning eleven. Imagine being a friend of Lin-Manuel Miranda, the writer of the acclaimed musical, early on in his creative writing process.

> *Lin-Manuel Miranda: "Hey, can you look over this rough draft for me?"*
>
> *Friend: "Cool. Sure. What is it?"*
>
> *Lin-Manuel Miranda: "Oh, it's just something I've been working on. It's about Alexander Hamilton."*
>
> *Friend: "It's about Hamilton? Like the guy who wrote the 'Federalist Papers'?"*
>
> *Lin-Manuel Miranda: "Yea, that's the guy. It's a musical."*
>
> *Friend: "A musical about the founding father Alexander Hamilton?"*
>
> *Lin-Manuel Miranda: "Yea, yea. It's a hip-hop musical. Can you let me know your thoughts?"*

Imagine what the friend must have been thinking. Imagine if Miranda ignored his passion and didn't create the musical he wanted. He didn't see that things *have to be that way*. He saw what he wanted to see and let his creativity carry him.

Take those risks! Take a page out of Miranda's book and thousands of writers before him. Try out a new plot-twist in your novel. Write an essay about your childhood experiences. Write a poem about the flowers in your backyard. See the world as you want it to be, not as it currently is. Then write about it.

See the world as you want it to be, not as it currently is.

There is always room to love more.

This is a great motto to live by. Your friends and family, and even strangers you meet on the street, will appreciate the love. However, I want you to implement this into two aspects of your writing.

First, always remember what initially inspired you to start writing. What motivated you to pick up the proverbial pen to put words down on paper? Maybe there were visions of grandeur and fame, but there are plenty of ways to chase that without sweating over a book, essay or poem. Our culture seems to always be looking for the next new reality star; you can probably chase fame easier that way, than by writing.

More than likely, you didn't start writing for the purpose of a foolish get-rich-quick scheme. You had a passion for it. You had a story bubbling up inside you that could no longer be contained. You had a love for writing. Always go back to that love. Especially on the days when you're scrambling for the motivation to sit down and do it. Always remember to love the process, then dip your pen into the ink of your love of writing.

Second, if you are writing a story where you are developing characters, apply this tip to each character you want to bring to life. Love your characters more. I mean literally. Have passion for them. Have hopes, dreams, fears, hate, anger, jealousy, excitement, and compassion. Love your characters as if they are your family and friends. Your readers will feel it when you have passion for your characters. Love them more each time you write about them. It will come through on the page.

If you're sitting there thinking that your writing doesn't have characters because you're not writing fiction, think again. All writing has characters that need to be loved. If you're writing a memoir, you need to learn to love the younger self you're writing about. If you're writing an essay or article about the state of the world, love the people affected, love the state or country impacted, love the planet that needs changing. If you're writing a self-help book, focus on each person you're writing the book for and lean in and love them.

Learn to love your characters deeply and your writing will jump off the page. Readers will take notice.

Be quick to show compassion and empathy.

T his is something we all need to do in our daily lives regardless of writing. Research shows that people who are more prone to being compassionate have a happier disposition and feel more fulfilled. Compassionate people tend to have more meaningful connections with others. They have a stronger sense of life purpose. Studies have shown this to be true. Lest you think this is just a touchy-feely piece of advice, you should know that it's been reported that the Chicago Cubs incorporated compassion and empathy training into their daily routines in 2016 when they won the baseball World Series for the first time in 108 years. There's concrete, practical gains to being compassionate and empathetic.

But what does this mean for us writers?

Every writer, whether you're on your fifteenth book or struggling to put together your first, has been in the situation of trying to figure out what happens next. Sometimes the story and plot lines flow out like a gushing waterfall of beautiful verses. Other times, it feels like tumbleweeds rolling through the empty highways of our brain.

When you find yourself suffering from the clichéd writer's block, take this advice to heart. Put yourself into your character's shoes. Show compassion and empathy.

> *em·pa·thy ('empəTHē/) noun- the ability to understand and share the feelings of another.*

What is your lead character feeling? Get yourself into his or her state mind. Put yourself in a place where you can understand and feel everything that your character is going through. It's the skill of the great writer. It's not simple, but it's necessary, and it does wonders to get the words flowing out of you again.

Writer's block? Put yourself into the shoes of your hero. Truly empathize with what she is experiencing.

While we're here talking about writer's block, let me share a few more tried and true methods I use to get out of the quagmire that plagues every writer I know. It is a rite of passage for the serious writer. If you have encountered writer's block, then you know you're doing something right. Whether you're writing a novel, a memoir, poems, or music, every writer suffers from it. Here are six Tips I find useful for writer's block.

Six Tips for Writer's Block

1. Shut Down

Distraction is the enemy of the writer. I find it difficult to write while other webpages and apps are open. I shut them down—email, Twitter, Facebook, all of it. I turn them off and focus on the task at hand—writing.

2. Have Multiple Projects

Having more than one project to focus on is extremely beneficial when faced with writer's block. You may be tired of writing about a particular character in your novel. You may be writing a memoir and find a certain event in your life is emotionally taxing. Put that project down for the day and move on to another one that you're pursuing. It doesn't have to be a formal project that will ever see the light of day. It can simply be writing poems, a letter, or even journaling.

3. Jump Around

There's a tendency to think we have to write our story the way our readers will read it—from beginning to end—but we don't have to follow a linear progression. Jump Around. If you know your novel needs to get from point A to B, but you're not quite sure how to get there, don't worry. Move on to point B and come back to fill in the details later. This will provide you with the creative luxury of exploring different parts of your story on any given day. It will free you from the burden of being stuck on a particular scene or plot point. You will be heavily editing your writing later on anyway, so you can fill in the holes another day.

4. Block Off Time to Write

We've discuss this in a number of the early Creative Writing Tips, but it's such an important thing to remember if you want to be a serious writer. It's an invaluable way to push through writer's block, too. There are always dozens of reasons that keep us from writing. When my wife was pregnant with our first child, my writing time decreased considerably, (as I'm sure you fellow parents can commiserate). I needed to block off time to sit and write. Early mornings, nap times, or late at night have been my primary writing hours. Even if you don't have young kids, or a day job, or other time commitments at all, we are all still prone to procrastination. Blocking off time to write forces you to create a writing habit, which will help long-term if you want to take writing seriously.

5. Just Write

Once you have time blocked off, just write. You may be excited and have a creative spark, which makes writing easy. Most often, we need to force ourselves to *just write*. Again, a lot will be changed or tossed out during the editing process. I have pages upon pages left on the cutting room floor. But I would have never found the pages of my book that were actually published if I didn't force myself to just write when I had time blocked off.

6. Decompress

Sometimes powering through writer's block is the solution. The old 'write your way out of it' philosophy. Other times, what's needed is to disconnect from your writing completely. Going for a long walk or socializing with friends can help. If the goal is to "unblock" your creative mojo, though, I find doing something else creative will do the trick. Maybe you like painting, or arts and crafts, or cooking. For me, I enjoy music. I find listening to or playing music is just what I need to release my creative ideas from the shackles of writer's block. When I'm stuck, I pick up my guitar and play. Sure enough, something clicks in my brain and ideas start flowing again.

6 Tips for Writer's Block

1. Shut down.

2. Have multiple projects.

3. **Jump around.**

4. **Block off time to write.**

5. **Just write.**

6. **Decompress.**

Take a step back and adjust your mindset.

T here are times when the thoughts and ideas that we want to write are right there in our mind's eye, but when we sit down, the words don't come. We're not at a loss of what to write, instead we find it painstakingly difficult to get the brilliant concepts in our heads onto the paper. We sit down with great ideas and then nothing comes out, or what does come out pales in comparison to what we wanted to write, so we delete it immediately.

If you're anything like me, you may be inclined to beat yourself up about poor writing or feel guilty about being unable to execute your ideas. If you're like me, you'll think it's a failure that you can't find the right words. Don't be like me though. Let's be better.

Instead of thinking in terms of failures and successes, think in terms of results. Why did I produce this result? How can I produce a different one? This will allow you to remove your emotion, stress and disappointment of the situation, and be able to think more clearly. When I adjust my mindset, and think in terms of results instead of failure, I think more clearly and make more rational decisions.

"There is no such thing as failure. There are only results."

-Tony Robbins.

Once you're in an adjusted mindset of focusing on results, take a different approach. If the right words aren't flowing from your brain onto the paper, one tried and true method to try is writing-prompts. You can find plenty of prompts online, or maybe just randomly pull a book off your shelf and write about the first sentence you read. How about taking a line from a song you like or a conversation you overheard? Or maybe just use the writing the prompt "I have nothing to write about" and write that line over and over until eventually, something will stream out of you. The idea is to keep the pen moving no matter what. And don't worry if nonsense comes out. Sometimes we need to empty the crammed thoughts that are pent up in our heads to make way for something else to pour out.

Let's try it:

I have nothing to write about.
I have nothing to write about.
I have nothing to write about.
I have nothing to write about

And neither do you,
But if we sit here long enough
The words will come through

That was unplanned and just using the writing prompt "I have nothing to write about." Words started to come through my head and find their way onto the paper. Try it on for size the next time the right words aren't flowing.

Take in the beauty of nature. Look around you. Don't take it for granted.

The best writers observe, everyone knows that. The mistake inexperienced writers often make is observing only for the purpose of writing about it. This causes them to miss important moments. They're observations are biased by their desire to find something interesting on which to write. The irony is that they become too focused on finding something worthwhile to write about that they miss what's happening around them.

Instead, just be. Sit with the world around you and take in its beauty.

Nature has a number of physical and mental benefits that are essential to writers. It has been shown to boost creativity. Spending time in nature is proven to reduce stress. Studies show that being in nature can cause a mental shift in our perception of time. There's a sense of time moving slower, which creates the feeling of having an abundance of it. Being in nature even improves memory and brain function.

Observe the world with passion.

Absorb the beauty around you.

Make sure that spending time in nature is an important part of your weekly or monthly diet. It will benefit your writing, improve your creativity, reduce your stress, and expand your ability to examine the world with insight. The best writers describe the scene that lay before them. That's because they are constant observers. Witness the world with passion and with both eyes wide open.

Take in the beauty of mankind. Look around you and see how wonderful your neighbor can be.

N ow that you're soaking in the beauty of nature, take a moment to see and feel the splendor of the people around you.

As we explored in Tip 11, the best writers are empathetic. Empathy means we can passionately feel another's pain and joy. The most captivating writers know this. They take it all in and find a way to translate that to the page.

Empathetic people feel another's pain and taste their joy.

The best writers do, too.

Share a laugh with your neighbor today. Hug your loved ones. Opening your heart to the world's pain and joy will make you a better writer, one that evokes a stir of emotion in your reader. Don't stop there either. Show empathy toward the jerk that cut you off this morning. Have compassion toward that rude woman who scowled at you on the street. Maybe she had a particularly bad morning. Who knows what tragedy has befallen on her life? It's easy to empathize with the person you love dearly, but true kindness extends toward even those whom you dislike. And quite honestly, an excellent writer intimately understands this. The world isn't black and white. A writer's job is to lay out all the complexities of world, to find beauty even in the ugly. It makes for a far more textured and compelling work.

Enjoy music.

I f you find your writing is becoming stale, sit back from time to time and enjoy music. I mean that quite literally. I want you to *enjoy music*. It has a way of seeping into the soul more viscerally than any other form of art. Let music inspire the words you are writing.

> **"Without music, life would be a mistake."**
>
> **-Friedrich Nietzsche**

In Daniel J. Levitin's book *This is Your Brain on Music,* he describes the brain as having two primary modes: (1) paying attention closely and (2) mind-wandering. It is believed that most creativity happens when we are in mind-wandering mode. This shouldn't be surprising. When do you usually stumble upon your best ideas? If you're like me, it's not when we are laser focused on a task, but instead, when we're in thoughtful, unorganized contemplation. It's during these times that our brains will connect two seemingly disparate things and a spark of creativity will occur to bridge them.

There are plenty of ways to get yourself into mind-wandering mode, and music is one of the most sure-fire ways to get there. As Levitin says, "Music is one of the most exquisitely effective ways of allowing you to enter the mind-wandering mode."

If you want to tap into your creativity, listen to music you enjoy.

Sit back and bask in the effortlessness of listening. It will unlock more creative potential in your writing. Don't worry about what the music is other than whether _you_ like it. It doesn't have to be a classical Mozart piece or a superb cello solo by Yo-Yo Ma. It can be that Taylor Swift song that lifts your spirits. It just needs to be something you enjoy.

I believe in this tip so much that I don't just listen to music almost every single time I'm writing, but I also wrote a story in my book _Pieces Like Pottery_ where each portion of the story is written with a particular song accompaniment in mind. The story itself is intended to be enhanced and the meaning of it, broadened by the songs selected for each part. Music is powerful.

Just in case you still aren't convinced, here are five additional ways in which music can enhance your writing.

Five (more) Ways Music Can Enhance Your Writing

1. Music Lowers Stress

We now know that music helps to open up creative avenues in the mind, but it also lowers stress levels just like spending time in nature does. A large number of studies have found that listening to music you enjoy will decrease levels of cortisol, the stress hormone, in the body. One 2002 study from the National Center for Biotechnology Information found that active participation in music produces a significant boost in the immune system.[1] Sing away, my friends!

2. Music Enhances Memory

In another study from 2013, researchers found that listening to pleasurable music activates areas of the brain implicated in

---

[1] Kuhn, Dawn. The effects of active and passive participation in musical activity on the immune system as measured by salivary immunoglobulin A (SIgA). J Music Ther. 2002 Spring; 39(1): 30-39.

emotion and reward.[2] They discovered that there's a correlation between listening to music and our ability to remember or memorize things. Want to be smarter? Want to increase your vocabulary? Listen to music.

3. Music Increases Verbal Intelligence

In a 2011 study published by the Department of Psychology at York University, researchers found that 90% of children had a significant increase in verbal intelligence after only one month of music lessons.[3] Sylvain Moreno proposed that there is a transfer effect that happens in our ability to understand language from music training, particularly for kids. What writer wouldn't like to have a better grasp of language?

4. Music Helps Sleep

A 2008 study showed that listening to music for 45 minutes before bed significantly improved sleep performance over those who just did their normal sleep routine.[4] I'm a terrible sleeper. I should take this one to heart.

5. Music Increases Happiness

---

[2] Gold, Benjamin P., Frank, Michael J., Bogert, Brigitte, & Brattico, Elvira. Pleasurable music affects reinforcement learning according to the listener. Front Psychol. 2013; 4: 541. Published online 2013 Aug 21. Doi: 10.3389/fpsyg.2013.00541

[3] Moreno, Sylvain, Bialystok, Ellen, Barac, Raluca, et al. Short-term music training enhances verbal intelligence and excutive function. Psychological Science. 2011; 22(11): 1425-1433.

[4] Harmat, Laszlo, Takacs, Johanna, Bodizs, Robert. Music improve sleep quality in students. Journal of Advanced Nursing. Published online 2008 April 18. Doi: 10.1111/j.1365-2648.2008.04602.x

Countless studies have shown that listening to music you enjoy releases dopamine in the brain. Dopamine is known as the "feel-good" or pleasure chemical. Increased dopamine levels cause an increase in excitement and joy. Music can increase dopamine levels. You get the picture.

> **"I don't sing because I'm happy, I'm happy because I sing."**
>
> **-William James**

Write with purpose.

N ow that you have music in your soul and empathy as the lens through which you peer, write with purpose. It sounds simple, but every writer struggles with this from time to time. Have a reason for putting that dinner scene in your book. Make sure that long soliloquy on the power of music has a purpose for being there. Be intentional about the words you choose in the poem you're writing. Don't just add words and scenes as filler. It has to have a purpose.

The purpose can be something as simple as you need a way to bring the plot from Point A to Point B. That's a great purpose. The key is to know exactly why you're writing it.

This will become even more important at the editing stage once you've completed initial drafts. If you're wondering what it adds to the story, cut it out. If you question why it's in there and YOU'RE THE ONE WHO WROTE IT, the reader is bound to wonder, too. Don't write just to have pages. Page and word counts are nonsense. Don't fixate on them. It will take away from your purpose and diminish the impact of your writing.

We've all read books like that, where the author seems to be repeating himself. In a self-help book, it's just the same point over and over. In a thriller, it's the same action scene three or four different times described in a slightly different way. Sometimes I think the publisher pushed for a longer book and the author was trying to make that happen.

Don't be that author. Make sure you know why you're writing what you're writing.

Know why you're writing every paragraph. Write with purpose.

Not everything you do has to have *a purpose*. Folly can be quite satisfying.

"**B**ut you just said to write with purpose! Now you're saying DON'T?!"

Not quite. Write with purpose, but your writing doesn't always have to have *a purpose*.

Let me equate this to life to try and elucidate the distinction, then we can see how it applies to writing. In life, we shouldn't just wander through our days without striving or fighting for something. We need to have goals. And purpose. However, every moment of every single day does not need to be chock full of distinct reasons for that moment. Sometimes you just need to look at the trees because you want to. Sometimes you need to dance just to dance. I have the most fun dancing my way up the stairs with my two young kids, for no reason at all. Kids or no kids, try it. You might thank me later!

So, what does this mean for us writers? I just finished saying to cut out parts of your writing that are superfluous. Don't have something in your content just to have more words or pages.

BUT...

If you feel like writing something different, just do it. You can cut it out in the editing process if it doesn't enhance or strengthen your work. Just write it. Don't worry if it's any good or if it makes sense yet.

That's how you get better as a writer. Try something on for size. Move that furniture around. You can always move it back. There's no reason not to try it. Even try writing things that may be casual side projects from the core writing you're doing. If you're feeling stuck on the book you're working on, sit and write something else for 30 minutes. Write about the beauty of a painting you love. Write a kid's poem about GI Joes. Write fan fiction about Harry Potter. Write whatever your heart darn well pleases. Dive into that folly for bit. That's one of the privileges of being a writer—you can write whatever you're inspired to write.

When you're ready to publish your work, everything written should have a reason to be there. When you're writing, be frivolous. It's the one place you can be!

Delve into the privilege of being a writer. Write with folly.

Your ambition means nothing without execution. Find the right editor.

The act of writing in and of itself is a monumental endeavor. I commend you for the words you have already written and the words you are going to write. To take ideas from your head and put them out onto the page, takes incredible passion and dedication. Well done!

Your work also needs another set of eyes. You need a trusted editor. I know, the editing process is a dreaded process for most writers, but it is just as important, and sometimes more so, than the writing process itself. Even the best writers need editors. Don't make the mistake of thinking you can go it alone.

Find an editor. Simple as that. Your work cannot thrive without strong edits.

You need to find someone who intuitively understands the story you're telling, the intonations, the rhythm, and the heart. Find an editor who goes beneath the grammar and correcting of typos. Leave that to the proofreaders. You need someone who 'gets it' and who won't impose their own agenda. An editor's job is to sift deep beneath the story with heightened sensitivity and attention to flow, repetition, wordiness, sentence structure, 'show don't tell,' and whether or not the message has impact while staying true to the spirit of the content. Find an editor who understands your work to its core.

I can't stress how important the right editor will be for you in your writing process. An editor is there to build your confidence when and if it falters. Your editor must know how to evoke your authentic self to come forward; to distill and refine *your* unique voice. They are there to be captivated by your style and enhance it; not alter it, but to highlight it to the magnitude of its beauty.

"I'm all for the scissors. I believe more in the scissors than I do in the pencil."

-Truman Capote

You can write and write and write until the end of time, but without a strong editor you trust, your work will probably suffer in its execution. You may have tremendous words written down, but your editor will help finalize it into something seamless. Don't wait until the end of your book or article or whatever you're writing to find an editor. Take advantage of having the support and fresh set of eyes and skill to support you along the way. The last thing you want is to finally reach the finish line after months, or even years, only to find it needs way more reworking than you thought. Having your editor there as an advocate can nip the inevitable mistakes in the bud and save you from the arduous task of going back through what you thought was complete. I am lucky to have an editor I trust. This book would never have taken the shape it did without having her involved early in the process.

In the end, though, trust your instincts. Put your ego aside and listen to everything your editor has to say, but if you ultimately don't like the suggested changes, trust that. Your editor is important, essential even, in the process, but the work is ultimately yours. Trust yourself and the vision you have for your writing.

Remember to read, and something more than a blog. Pick up a book from time to time.

I know this seems obvious, but if it's so obvious, why aren't more people doing it? I had what some called a little bit of a rant on my website (www.nothinganygood.com). I have seen a mindset amongst some of the author community that bothers me to no end. There is a sentiment I encounter far too often where writers say they can't read anything right now because they don't want it to influence their writing.

Why is this a thing? It is the silliest possible response to the question, "What are you reading?" Writing and reading are the two best ways to become a better writer. Why would you cut out one of those avenues? I have a hard time believing reading George Saunders will negatively impact your genius humor. I doubt you'll need to avoid reading George Orwell because your unconscious mind will inadvertently steal ideas from him.

"Writer's need to read."

-Ian McEwan

Reading will most certainly impact your writing—POSITIVELY. If you're an athlete, the best way to get better is to practice the sport and watch game film. If you're a dancer, dancing and watching what others do propels you to become a better dancer. If you're a painter, painting and studying other's paintings is the best way to learn. Writing is no different. You need to write and also study other authors through reading. It will inspire ideas and help you understand areas where you can improve in your writing. It will diversify your vocabulary as well. I constantly learn new words when reading.

I get the idea of not having as much time to read as you would like, but the fact that you can't read while you're writing because you'll unknowingly steal ideas is preposterous to me. Please don't be one of those writers. Read often. Read everything you can get your hands on. And not just on your phone. If you want to be a good writer, read, Read, READ.

"If you don't have time to read, you don't have time (or the tools) to write. Simple as that."

-Stephen King

Save your writing.

I always encourage writers to save their writing. I have old notebooks of writings and poems that date back to my teenage years. I've saved word docs from over 10 years ago with stories and articles that I never polished and finalized. I keep these because I never know when I'll be writing something and remember that I have an old anecdote, story, or paragraph from years back that will fit perfectly into what I'm writing now. Always save your writing, friends. An old piece might end up being a great launching point for a new one.

I used to run an email list called *The Dailie Break*. Unoriginal, right? Well, it was fifteen years ago. It was before the internet took shape in its current form. There wasn't social media yet and even blogs weren't a thing. (Can you imagine?) While a daily email wasn't an earth-shattering idea, there also wasn't a lot of them going around. I ran it for nearly seven years. With no intention of doing anything more than sending it out to a few people, the list expanded exponentially from five original subscribers. It grew by word of mouth, quite to my surprise.

The point is not to share a trip down memory lane with you, though. When I knew that *The Dailie Break* had run its course and I was done with it, I sent one final email to my readers. I had no intention other than to offer a heartfelt email that day. I saved it, and to this day, I'm still not sure why.

Years later, when I was writing the short story *Expect Dragons*, I sat down to write Mr. Smith's 40 Tips for College and Life. Wracking my brain writing and rewriting them, I remembered the old email I sent and a few sentences in there that I enjoyed. I dug it up and went through it. I had no idea, nor any intention of using this email later on in my writing. It's not very good. The grammar is poor and there are errors that need to be edited. But I had the wherewithal to save the darn thing and I was glad I did.

Here is a portion of that email from over 10 years ago in all its poorly written glory (some of it will look familiar):

7 years ago, this May, The Dailie Break was born at the back-corner cubicle of a law firm in downtown Minneapolis. As a young 22-year-old, I was full of excitement and energy, interning for a law firm, waiting tables, and playing in endless Texas Hold 'Em tournaments at Canterbury Downs. I was the quintessential adolescent male. Before you think interning for a law firm at the age of 22 is impressive, let me assure you, it was not. My job consisted of driving to an old warehouse in a mini-van, loading up boxes of old files, sorting through them to enter

them into an electronic database and shredding the ones the partners signed off to be shred. Not very glamorous.

The significance of this summer in 2004 is that it was my first desk job. Like anyone sitting down at a desk for the first time, it sucked. So, I sent an email out to a few of my brothers and friends declaring that I'd send a daily email out in order to break up the monotony of the work day. I sent the first email without knowing where it may lead. I never thought it would last nearly seven years. The first few editions were sent out to make readers laugh. Then a writer I enjoy, who greatly impacted black culture in sports in America, passed away; so I provided his post-9/11 article to readers. Somehow, word spread like whatever the opposite of wild fire is and TDB grew. We saw horrible tsunamis, school shootings, floods, earthquakes, wars, deaths and murders. We saw presidential elections, championships, Nobel prizes, births and weddings.

The world moves fast and time goes quickly, so TDB was created to remind us to stop sometimes—to make us laugh, think, and sometimes, cry. Life gets in the way of living and we need to be reminded of that from time to time. That's what TDB aimed to do. It was created to make us think outside the box. Not everyone thinks the way you do, (or I do); that's something to be embraced, not shunned. It was created to make us realize, not everything has to have a point, (hence the baffling spelling of the name). In its development over seven years, it became exactly the thing it was intended to destroy—monotony. So, unfortunately, it is time. But I will leave you with this.

Have a routine, but avoid being routine. Life's too short to not seize the opportunities with which we are presented. Always take the chance to do what you love when it comes along. Question authority. Question those who question authority. We are all intelligent, thoughtful individuals. Don't let others tell you something *has to be that way*. It doesn't. The world is far too complex for it to *have to be that way*. Share laughter. There's far too much that's funny out there to take yourself and others too seriously. Share tears. There's far too much pain and hurt out there not to take others struggles seriously. Decide what you believe, know who you are and live accordingly. Don't apologize for that. But if you realize later on that you were wrong, admit it. Ask for forgiveness. Maya Angelou has a great quote: "If I'd known better, I'd done better." We can only do the best we know how, but there's no excuse for not striving to attain the know-how. And there's certainly no excuse for not doing better once we have it.

Finally, be kind. Kindness can change things far beyond our wildest dreams. They say that absence makes the heart grow fonder, but it's kindness that makes the heart grow softer.

Thank you and farewell.

That's the email I sent out the day that list ended. Some of it might look familiar, no?

These are partially the same edited 40 Tips you're reading now. I may have never finished them had I not kept that email from years ago. Save your writing! This is only one example of many where I've dug up an old piece and used it in the perfect spot later. You never know when you might need that scene, quote, essay, or character description again. Save it.

An old piece of writing can be a friend to a new piece. Hang on to everything you write.

It's easy to doubt. Don't be easy. Hold on to faith and hope.

I know the feeling. Whether you're trying to finish your first novel or your fifth, every writer knows about that constant, nagging doubt inside your head.

This book isn't any good.
I'll never finish it.
I'll never get published.
No one will ever read my book.

Don't listen to those doubts. Stay the course. Continue to write because you love it. Hold on to the hope of your dreams. Have faith that if you continue to work hard at writing, you will in fact find that book finished, that essay published, that project completed. It's easy to doubt! Let go of its hold and grab the reigns of your aspirations.

As authors, we are often asked, "Why did you first start writing?" or "Why do you write?" The typical answer that most authors give, myself included, is some sort of anecdote about a deep-rooted love of writing or a long-held passion for storytelling that we've possessed since we were young. And while this is in fact true, it doesn't seem to get to the heart of the matter.

We do enjoy telling stories. Taking a passionate life event or a spectacular action sequence and committing it to the page in an effective and compelling manner, is the great challenge of the writer. The goal is to communicate to the reader. Trying to accomplish this in a way that is captivating, is what all writers seek. But the question still remains—*Why do we write?*

The fact that we enjoy storytelling doesn't necessarily shed light on why we write. There seems to be something much more fundamental to the human experience that compels us.

Why do you write?

Decide now and remind yourself every day.

Good writing is proven through the ability to write well, rather than the ability to come up with great ideas. A fine writer can compose a good story because she has good ideas that are the foundation of that story. But great writers are able to take the most mundane subjects and write marvelously about them.

The distinguished writer G.K. Chesterton, for example, has written essays on topics as banal as boredom and resting, and they are extremely thought-provoking and entertaining essays. Good writing doesn't _need_ a good story. On the other hand, poor writing can destroy a great idea.

The key for great writers is that they can capture a reader's attention with the simplest of subjects just because their writing is extraordinary. When first starting out, too many writers have an interesting idea or a persuasive plot line, and they simply begin to write. They fail to realize that a persuasive plot line does not make a good writer. As writers, we need to learn to write well and worry about the interesting ideas later.

The goal of the writer is to communicate to the reader, whether through a story, a novel, an essay, a poem, or any other form of written word. As writers, we're trying to communicate, and great writers have perfected this mode of communication.

The human species is a communicative being and, as such, we are all searching for people with whom to communicate. Whether it is with our family and friends, our coworkers and neighbors, or just the barista at the local coffee shop, we long to express even just a little part of ourselves. We yearn to be seen, and to be understood. Because of this, we strive to see others as well. Call it an extension of the Golden Rule—we try to understand those around us because we, ourselves, want to be understood.

At the root of things, this is why we write. We hunger to see and be seen; to understand and be understood. We write to preserve a memory, to sustain a thought. Without it, we fear we will become forgotten.

Always remember why you write. Remind yourself of it early and often. If you can hold onto this, your doubts will fade away. You will always have faith and hope nearby. And along with your faith and hope, you can strive for your dreams.

"Every single person you will ever meet wants to know: 'Do you see me? Do you hear me? Does what I say mean anything to you?'"

-Oprah Winfrey

Walk barefoot through the grass.

This one is simple. Enjoy the little things. Take time for yourself. Always remember to take a break.

It seems obvious, but you'd be surprised how often we neglect nourishing ourselves. Remember to do this. If you love to run, go running. If you meditate or pray, set aside time for that. If you love to play an instrument, play.

You will be far more productive when you care for yourself. If the only question in front of you is, "Should I write at this very moment or should I make time for myself because I'm stressed," scientific research answers resoundingly that you should take time for yourself. It's not even close.

In Arianna Huffinton's book *Thrive,* she presents that there's overwhelming research on how self-care profoundly affects our productivity. "We think, mistakenly, that success is the result of the amount of time we put in at work, instead of the quality of time we put in," Huffington writes. And then later on, "If you take care of your mind, you take care of the world."

Your body and mind run at a higher performance level if you take care of them. Make self-care a priority.

There is a quote that I love. I've seen it attributed to a number of people, including Saint Francis de Sales, Saint Teresa of Avila, Deepak Chopra, and Saint Thérèse of Lisieux among others. (I always thought it was Saint Thérèse of Lisieux, but after trying to confirm who said it first, it's entirely unclear to me now who actually wrote this and what the actual quote is. There seems to be much disagreement on this.)

So rather than providing a quote in error and attributing it to the wrong person, I'll provide the quote I've heard and have always enjoyed. You can attribute it to someone that is much wiser than I, which is almost everyone.

"Pray an hour every day, unless you're busy. If you're busy, pray two hours."

This is beautiful and profoundly true. We cannot draw from an empty well. Fill yourself up and replenish. It makes for lush, fertile writing.

We discussed earlier that the best thing you can do as a writer is to actually sit down and write, and this remains true. You need to take time to actually write, which requires commitment. I am adamant that this is the most important element for someone who wants to be a serious writer. If you want to take your writing to the next level, carve out the time for it.

Once you've become disciplined, whether that's every day or a number of times a week, the next step is to actually write during that allotted time. In today's media-at-our-fingertips-age, it's easy to get distracted by the latest reality show, or your friend's pics of Paris, or that book about 40 Creative Writing Tips. (I know it's bad business, but if you're supposed to be writing right now, stop reading this book and go write! What are you doing?! I'll be here when you finish writing for the day.)

In my own writing, I've discovered I must write during the time I've allotted for it. Sometimes the words feel stale and clunky. Other times, sentences string together like poetic beauty. It doesn't matter. When you're supposed to be writing, just write. Worry about the quality during the editing process.

BUT...

And here's the but...

Again, if the only question in front of you is, "Should I write at this very moment or should I take time for myself because I'm stressed?" You should take time for yourself. Without question, replenish. Your body and mind need it for peak performance.

Take time for yourself. Enjoy the little things. Walk barefoot through the grass.

"Pray an hour every day, unless you're busy. If you're busy, pray two hours."

Smile.

T ry it. Seriously, go ahead and do it right now. Close your eyes, take a deep breath, think about why you love writing, and smile.

Research shows that the simple physical act of smiling can provide tremendous health benefits, regardless of whether you were actually feeling happy when you started smiling. In his 2006 best seller *Stumbling on Happiness*, Harvard psychology professor Daniel Gilbert explains that the act of smiling can trigger the release of neuropeptides and serotonin, which can have a dramatic impact on your mental health. It can relieve stress and increase your ability to relax.

Don't smile because you're happy, smile because you want to be happy.

The revered Buddhist monk Thích Nhất Hạnh has a wonderful quote. "Sometimes your joy is the source of your smile, but sometimes your smile can be the source of your joy."

Remember why you started writing in the first place. If you began writing because you threw away all your years of actuarial schooling and thought you could become far richer as an author, then maybe you should be frowning. Unless you have the writing lottery ticket, that's a tough reason for becoming an author.

But if you began your journey as an author for the same reason I, and many of my author-friends did, because there are stories constantly percolating in your brain, words and thoughts burning inside you ready to leap out onto the page, because you feel fulfilled when you write. If this is you, then take a moment right now to remember why you write. Take a moment and smile just because you're a writer.

Remember why you started writing and smile because you're a writer.

We have spent the first half of the book focusing on writing. How to put ourselves in the best position to put meaningful and thoughtful words down on paper. How to avoid common pitfalls of unsuccessful writers. How to find the voice inside of us and to remain focused on our goals as writers. We are about to spend the next tips exploring getting involved in the writer community, publishing, and marketing.

If you are working on finishing your first work, good for you! Stay focused on that. Don't get distracted by the writing community, publishing, marketing, or anything else. Make your way through the next tips to expand your knowledge of things to come, but don't become distracted or stressed by the next stages. Focus on your beautiful writing.

And before we move on, let's stop and smile together. Just smile.

Don't be afraid to be alone. Everyone knows: "Not all who wander are lost." Few realize: Not all who are alone are lonely.

B eing a writer can be a lonely existence. It can also be tremendously rewarding, fulfilling, and surprisingly communal. Don't mistake the fact that you have to be alone to think or write, with being lonely. You have a wonderful community of authors alongside you. Remember that.

If you're not on Goodreads, that's a good place to start. If you're not familiar, Goodreads is a social media network with hundreds of thousands of readers and writers. There are genre specific groups for everyone. Are you interested in vampire books? There's a group for that. Apocalyptic adventures? They have that too. I'm positive you'll find your niche amongst the Goodreads community.

Be alone, but don't be lonely. There's a huge writing community here to support you.

Beyond Goodreads, there are plenty of other options online. Find places that fit well for you, but be selective. There's a mantra I tell myself regularly: "You can do anything. You can't do everything." Be selective about where you utilize social media. Each platform is different. Twitter can help you reach new readers, while Facebook can drive more traffic to your website. Instagram and Pinterest can help you build a brand, if that's what you're going for. This is just the tip of the iceberg of social media options. Figure out what works best for you and focus on those one or two platforms. Personally, I have my website at *www.Nothinganygood.com* that has a good following and community around it. I also get involved on Twitter and a bit on Facebook.

Remember real-life interactions, too. Search writing groups and book clubs in your own city. Venture out into the community. Get involved with your local libraries and bookstores. Here in Portland, Oregon, there's an amazing writing and reading festival every year called Wordstock. It combines indie presses, booksellers, and authors in a wide variety of exhibits, panels, presentations, and events. You may not have Wordstock in your hometown, but I'm sure there are options to get involved in the writing community. Seek them out.

The physical act of writing may be an endeavor you undertake alone, just you, your thoughts, and the blank page in front of you. That doesn't mean it must be a lonely experience. Be alone, but don't be lonely. We're with you!

Share your excitement. People who hold that against you are most likely projecting their own feelings of inadequacy.

This one is particularly difficult for me. I'm not sure why that is. Maybe someday a therapist can help me better understand my feelings of anxiety and fear, but we'll leave that for another day. Or another book! I find it difficult to express my excitement about certain things I love. For a long time, writing was one of them.

I've loved writing since I was a boy. However, I never had an outlet for it; or a writing mentor who could help me channel that excitement productively and creatively. I used to write primarily in private. I have many essays from my younger days written in journals and on loose-leaf paper that the world will never see. I have countless words that have been deleted or thrown into the garbage over the years. I have a half-finished novel that I wrote in college and is lost on a stolen laptop somewhere. You'll have to take my word for it, though, because no one will ever see most of it. I was just never comfortable sharing my love of writing.

Share your love for the craft that is uniquely yours.

A number of years ago I decided to dip my toes into the proverbial waters of writing publicly. My wife and I had a blog—a very well-regarded and followed blog, I might add—about the joys and struggles of marriage and life. It was a He-Says-She-Says blog about one topic that we chose every week. (It's been almost a decade since our last post and we still have people wondering if we'll ever bring it back. If you're curious, it's called Buris On the Couch. You can still find the archives if you care to: *burisonthecouch.wordpress.com.*)

At the time, I still wasn't comfortable making our identities entirely clear other than the name of the blog. Those close to us knew it was us, but many of our readers didn't know who we were. Our names weren't used and I never wanted pictures posted. It was my own fear of sharing my excitement for writing. I'm sure that it robbed the blog of being everything it could have been. I wasn't allowing myself to find that REAL YOU inside of me. Despite the strong reception, people often felt they couldn't fully connect with us and that was because I was afraid to let myself be vulnerable and share my love of writing.

Finally, realizing that I wasn't getting any younger, and with the kind and constant encouragement from my wife, a number of years ago, I decided to share my passion for writing more vocally. I finalized *Pieces Like Pottery* and started my website for indie authors, *www.Nothinganygood.com*. I have no regrets.

I tell you this to encourage and provide an instructive anecdote. Don't be like me. Share your excitement for writing with the world. Sure, people have ridiculed and mocked my enjoyment of the craft, but that's their issue, not mine. That's their own projections of inadequacy. I'm not going to own that for them. I did that long enough in my early years.

Use my shortcomings as a tale of inspiration. If you love what you just wrote, share it. If you love your book, your essay, your poem, share it. Enjoy what you're writing just for the simple fact that you're writing it. Share your love for the craft that is uniquely yours.

Laugh hard, disparage slowly, and forgive quickly.

L ike most of these tips, the next two are wonderful advice to follow in our everyday lives, but they are smart advice for us writers as well. There are three individual pieces of advice to consider in Tip 26 that I want you to contemplate in your author-efforts.

Let's take them one by one

Laugh Hard.

Don't forget to laugh, friends. Laugh hard and laugh often.

You're going to fall on your face as an author. Accept that fact now. When it happens (and it will happen), be ready to laugh at yourself and move on. Take it in stride. It says nothing about you as a person or as a writer. Learn every lesson you can from it.

You will encounter people that hate what you write. They will say unkind things about your writing. Be prepared for it and laugh it off as much as possible.

Don't believe me? My book *Pieces Like Pottery* has over 100 reviews on Amazon and the majority are 4 or 5 star ratings. I've been thrilled and humbled by the reception it received. Still, negative reviews come in, both in the form of Amazon and social media. Recently, someone had the following comment for me: "I didn't really get a chance to hate it, but the language threw me from the page before I could get to know the characters or story."

That sure sounds like a book I would hate! If I couldn't even read past the first bit of a book, I think it's safe to say I didn't like it. To say you didn't get the chance to hate it because…well…you stopped reading due to hating it that much, certainly sounds like you hated it! What'd I do? I thanked the reader for their thoughts and for considering my book. I laughed it off and moved on. Not everyone is going to like my writing and that's fine with me.

> **Learn to laugh. It will make your life as a writer much more enjoyable.**

Disparage Slowly.

Just like learning to laugh often, learn to use that laughter to uplift. You will encounter friends or family that playfully (or not so playfully) mock your endeavor to be a writer. The world is full of haters and you will encounter them. Publications, publishers, agents, and readers will reject your writing time and again. You will come face-to-face with writers who are more successful than you. Your inclination may be to react and strike back. Don't. Don't! Always encourage and uplift other writers and readers. There's no need to disparage others.

As writers, we get knocked to the ground a lot. Writing can have a way of beating us down. Take it all in stride and keep fighting for your goals. It will take a lot of persistence to get to where you want to go, but remove disparagement from your toolbox of things that you use to get you there. There's no need for it. And it certainly won't get you there.

Forgive Quickly.

If we're no longer disparaging people that may not understand our goals, or our writing, or the effort we've invested, the next step is to let it go entirely. Not only don't lash out at them, but actually forgive them. And forgive yourself if you have a momentary lapse of wanting to strike back. We all have those moments. Forgive and forgive quickly. You will be much better off. It will give you more time to focus on what you really want to be focusing on—your writing.

> **Every moment you spend refusing forgiveness is wasted energy deterring you from your goals.**

Eat fully, drink deeply, and remember to give often.

There are couple things I want us to take away from this tip. First, enjoy writing! All of it! Savor the writing process. Yes, even the editing.

I've said it before and I'll say it again later in the book because it's that important for all of us to remember. Never forget why you wanted to write in the first place. You had a story that you wanted (or needed) to tell. Everything else is just details on how to get there. That story is inside you and the writing, the editing, the rewriting, the re-editing, the publishing, is all a part of accomplishing the best version of that story. Enjoy it!

Drink deeply from the writing cup that sits in front of you. Eat fully from the feast of wonderful authors that have written before you. Relish in the process from beginning to end.

Second, always give back. Remember, there are other authors out there trying to find their way in a very difficult writing-world. There are others who struggle with the exact same thing you're struggling with now, or have in the past. Help those authors who need assistance. Offer advice. Post reviews. (Always post reviews!) Connect writers to other writers, cover designers, and editors who will help them. Hell, start a website aimed to help authors and aspiring writers if you feel so inclined. (Just don't call it www.*Nothinganygood.com*. That's taken!)

Remember to give often. The author community is a strong one. You will meet amazing people and many of them are incredibly generous with their resources. Be one of those people who give back.

Always give back. Remember that there are other authors out there trying to find their way, too.

Don't act like you know more than you do. There's no shame in admitting you don't know the answer.

Authors are very good at purporting to have all the answers. I suspect it's a combination of two things. First, the fear of failure. That constant looming fear of utter defeat. Authors are either afraid of failing, or they're lying about it.

There's a wonderful TED Talk by Jia Jiang titled "What I learned from 100 Days of Rejection." Look it up. It's a great watch and will help you in your battle with rejection and fear of failure. Jiang begins by sharing a time when he was six years old and felt rejected by his classmates. This moment stuck with him for decades and inspired his fascination with rejection, particularly why everyone is so afraid of it.

To overcome his fear, Jiang sought rejection out for 100 straight days. Have a look at some of his outlandish escapades:

- *Rejection 1: Borrow $100 from a Stranger;*
- *Rejection 2: Request a Burger Refill;*
- *Rejection 3: Ask for Olympic Symbol Doughnuts;*

Aren't those fantastic? I thoroughly enjoyed this TED Talk and feel it's a must-watch for every writer out there. We know rejection all too well. It comes with the territory. If you're struggling with the rejection that comes with being a writer, sit down and watch this video. If you haven't been rejected yet, watch the clip to help you prepare for that inevitable day.

> # You can be rejected without being a writer, but you can't be a writer without being rejected.

Jiang sought to desensitize himself to the shame and pain of rejection. This is a powerful idea. Shame can be absolutely debilitating. As Brené Brown writes in her bestselling book *Daring Greatly*, "Shame derives its power from being unspeakable."

So, let's speak about rejection more. There's nothing to be ashamed about. As writers, we have been and will continue to be rejected in one form or another. My first fiction book was rejected by over 100 publishers and agents before I decided to self-publish and watched it climb to bestseller status. I wear those rejection slips with pride. Wear yours with pride, too.

Don't let rejection define you. Let your reaction to rejection define you.

Now that we've covered the first reason that authors often pretend to know more than they do—fear of failure—let's look at the second reason. The second is the old *fake-it-til-you-make-it* ideology. I get the impression that a lot of authors pretend like the book-world is always shining its proverbial sun down upon them. Many authors feel the need to exude a certain level of success. This is particularly true on social media platforms like Facebook, Twitter, and Goodreads. Authors long for everyone to think they're making it as a writer and pretend thousands of readers are clamoring at their doorstep to read their next book. The truth is far less glamorous.

I fall victim to this from time to time, but there's no shame in admitting that we don't always know the answer. None of us have it all figured out. Hell, the book experts don't always have it figured out. I understand trying to be confident, but don't be afraid to ask questions about things you don't know. It'll be good for you in your development as writer.

It's OK to admit you don't know the answer to everything. It's OK to be an outsider. As writers, we should use this to our advantage. There are plenty of challenges not being "in the know," but there are also great advantages. In the tech world, those individuals who are ignorant about the status quo are considered outsiders. They are often the ones who disrupt the market with new innovations and displace the established market players. Writers are often considered to be outsiders. They write something brilliant and shake up what people deem to be excellent writing. William Blake, Emily Dickinson, J.D. Salinger, Cormac McCarthy, Dave Eggers, Ta-Nehisi Coates, Lin-Manuel Miranda...the list goes on. If there's something you don't know, ask questions and learn to use what you don't know to your advantage.

Ignorance sometimes frees us from the norms and expectations that can stifle creativity. In Jonah Lehrer's book *Imagine*, he explores, mainly through anecdote, how creativity often comes from outsiders who don't feel restrained by the unwritten rules of the trade. This is because they don't know those rules yet. (I realize that Lehrer's book was well-regarded for a short time, until it was revealed that he self-plagiarized and fabricated portions. However, the ideas he presents, at least in part, have merit and have stuck with me for years, particularly the idea that outsiders can bring the most creativity to the table.)

> **Ignorance can free us from the norms and expectations that stifle our writing creativity.**

If you're an indie author or self-published, then you're at a distinct disadvantage from the books published by the Big 5, particularly in the arenas of marketing and available capital. But it also puts you at a unique advantage to bring creative solutions to the table. You don't have to follow the unwritten rules that traditional publishers have created because, if you're like me, you don't know them. We're outsiders, so go ahead and be an outsider. Embrace your ignorance.

Don't act like you know less than you do. What you do know has great value. Share your knowledge.

N ow that we're in agreement that we're going to ask more questions and admit when we don't know all the answers, it's time to admit that there are some things we absolutely do know. Feel free to share the knowledge you have.

Honestly, I need to remind myself of this. I know it might not seem like it since I run a website aimed to support and help authors, but I am afraid to share my knowledge. Back in school, I was always the guy in the back of the class keeping his mouth shut. I did this all through college and law school. It's a disease of self-doubt. I'm plagued by it.

The only reason this book came into existence is because of reader encouragement. Many followers of *Nothinganygood.com* suggested I consolidate my writing tips and put them in a book. I listened. You have yourselves to thank, so a round of applause to you.

I remind myself daily to suck up my fear of being wrong about my knowledge and just share what I know. You should do the same. Put yourself out there. Share what you know.

Share your knowledge. Engage with the writing community.

Don't take yourself too seriously. Find the humor.

I can't say it enough, you started writing because you had a story to tell and you love to write. Don't ever forget why you started. Embrace the successes and the failures, and everything in between.

When I finished my first published book, I believed the best path to finding an agent and a publisher was to first get some of my writing published in a prestigious literary journal. I had been published in legal journals as a lawyer, online publications as a writer, and print journals as a photographer, but I never experienced the success of seeing one of my written *fiction* works published in a prestigious journal.

I set out on a plan to submit adapted stories to journals. I contacted over 100 journals in a 12-month period. You read that right. Over 100. (My definition of the term "prestigious journal" became flexible after the first 40 or so). Guess how many journals and magazines responded to me positively?

Exactly zero. None. Nada. Zilch. Zip.

I'm sure you can imagine my disappointment after all that effort. In one of my last-ditch attempts, I submitted to the University of St. Thomas, a liberal arts college in St. Paul, Minnesota. Their Summit Avenue Press published a photo of mine nearly two decades ago. My father is the longest tenured professor at the University. Two of my brothers were All American basketball players there. If I couldn't get published there, where could I get published? I might as well give up on this whole writing thing, right?

You know what I received as a response? A big fat, "No thanks."

Embrace the entire writing process, both the successes and the failures.

It was a form letter written by a junior in college replete with typos. It even included use of the term "BS." As in, "We had more submissions than we could print. This sounds like BS, but it's highly likely, since we had over 200 submissions and could only choose a handful for publication."

Highly likely? It either happened or it didn't. What do you mean 'highly likely?'

Here's how it ended:

"We in our limitless, faultless wisdom as undergraduate English majors who've completed three years of college

and thus never make mistakes failed to see the pedigree of your work. If this is the case, we hope you're not discouraged by this letter, and will instead take this as an opportunity to send your work to other magazines who will no doubt give it a better home."

While attempting to be humorous, this letter acted as a metaphorical kick in the nuts. A lifelong passion of mine was rejected by over 100 journals. A school to which my family has close ties responded to my submission with a poor attempt at cheekiness in a rejection letter. Ouch.

In the end, I had an option. I could take it personally and let it discourage me from my passion, or I could laugh. You already know which option I chose. All I could do was laugh. I had to. I shared the news with my wife and she laughed right along with me. There was no other choice in my mind. I had been rejected by college English students.

I'm glad I picked myself back up by laughing it off. I wouldn't have had the critical success that I've seen with *Pieces Like Pottery* if I didn't. If I couldn't laugh about it, I most likely would have given up on that first book. Or worse yet, I could have given up on writing entirely.

There's too much that's funny out there to take myself too seriously. I choose to see the humor in things. That's the only way I know.

You will, no doubt, find yourself in many stressful and disappointing situations as a writer. Always remember to take a step back, relax, and brush it off. It will do you wonders.

"I think that you have to believe in your destiny; that you will succeed, you will meet a lot of rejection and it is not always a straight path, there will be detours—so enjoy the view."

-Michael York

Share tears. There's far too much pain out there not to take others' struggles seriously.

I f there's anything I've learned in my journey as a writer, it's to laugh at myself and cry with others. This advice has served me well. Don't belittle another writer's pain or disappointment. They have struggled on a journey that may be identifiable to you, but it is uniquely their own. Sit with your fellow writers and share in their suffering. And even though I said not to take ourselves too seriously, it is important to feel your own pain too. If you're down and hurt and want to cry, let yourself cry. Don't belittle your own, or anyone else's feeling of defeat. Sit at the table with it, then after recognizing and accepting it, excuse yourself from the table. Lighten up so you can move along with your good endeavors.

There's no way to share tears, or joy, if there's no one around to share them with. As we discussed in Tip 24, get involved in your local writer and author communities on social media. There's some amazing people out there who know what it's like. You're here reading this book, so you have a leg up.

Once you make connections, be sincere and vulnerable with other authors. Someone else may be struggling with the rejection letter she just received. An author friend you met online may be finding it difficult to finish the book he's working on. Be there for them. Don't invalidate another writer's struggle. It is theirs, and it's real for them. Be the one they can lean on when they're losing faith. Help them release their self-doubt. Share tears and then lift each other up to forge on.

> **"There is no exercise better for the heart than reaching down and lifting people up."**
>
> **-John Holmes**

Be kind. They say that absence makes the heart grow fonder, but kindness makes the heart grow softer.

This applies to much more than just being a writer, but it is something more writers need to remember. Far too many of us forget the simple rule of kindness, particularly in the marketing and selling of our books.

Every author would love an ever-growing readership. Every writer would love hundreds of positive reviews. But recognize that people may not want to read your book. It's not an attack on you. They are busy and there are a lot of interesting things competing for their attention. I know it hurts that someone wouldn't want to read something you've spent years of thought and pain and sacrifice creating, but that hurt is yours, not theirs. Simply recognizing and processing your hurt will do wonders for you in being kind. It doesn't help projecting that hurt onto your potential readership.

Remember, not everyone will to like your book, essay, article, or poem. That's their right. After you publish, it's no longer yours. It's the readers. You have to be comfortable with that no matter how painful the result may be. That's the life of a writer.

Once you publish your work, it's no longer yours. It's the readers.

Someone on twitter the other day DM'd me saying they really enjoyed a quote of mine they saw. As you would expect, I was thrilled and grateful to hear that. I love feedback! I told this lovely woman, "It's a quote from my book. I would love to hear your thoughts on it if you happen to read it. No expectations!"

She responded, "Sorry, but I don't read books that have been cold-call pitched to me!"

Uh, Ok?

The cynical side of me wanted to give her a verbal eye roll or flex the boundaries of my vocabulary, but that's not a kind response. So, I refrained and remembered kindness.

I guess I sort of "pitched" her my book, in the loosest sense of the term, although I'm not sure about the cold-call part since she reached out to me. But maybe she gets contacted nonstop by authors to read their books. Maybe she's tired of seeing people's books and just wants to read whatever she damn well pleases, so my DM exchange with her got lumped in with everyone else that aggressively pesters her. I needed to see her side of things.

My response was much kinder than the cynical side of me wanted to be: "Have a wonderful day! I hope you're reading something excellent right now. All my best."

Kindness softens us. I saw a meme on Facebook the other day in beautiful bright colors that said, "In a world where you can be anything, be kind." Let's put that in our growing number of mantras to repeat. Be kind, be kind, be kind.

Want a book review? Be kind.

They said they won't review your book? Be kind.

Want new readers? Be kind.

They said they don't want to read your book? Be kind.

Point is, be kind.

Promote your writing smartly, not loudly.

Authors have a strange job description, especially indie authors and self-published authors. Being an author often involves many more job descriptions than being a writer. Authors have to understand and execute a variety of jobs, which often includes writing, editing, formatting, coding, and marketing. We are the jack of all trades in the writing world. There are plenty of places to fall down in this process, but it's the marketing efforts (or marketing flubs) that are the most visible. Now I'm no marketing expert, but I have learned a thing or two in my time as an indie author. Here are five common mistakes to avoid when marketing your book.

1. Buy My Book!

This is the most common and the most tired marketing effort used by authors. It seems to be a failure due to either one of two things. One, the author doesn't know how to market his book other than coming right out and screaming it, which I fear is probably often the case with many authors. It's difficult to come up with unique and creative ways to get the word out about your book, I get it. But screaming about it isn't going to get the results you want.

The other reason authors most likely do this is because they've confused the need for a *call-to-action* on their website with something that is acceptable on social media. The simplest way I can explain the difference is to bring this into a brick-and-mortar, real-world context. Imagine you are doing a book reading at a local bookstore. Having a stand with a placard that says "Get Your Copy Here" is great. That is acceptable. Approaching everyone in the bookstore with your book saying, "Buy my book!" is obnoxious. That is unacceptable.

> **Treat social media the same way you would the real world.**
>
> **Try to engage and interact. Don't always try to sell.**

2. Buy Me Book!

I struggle with this all the time. We are busy people and are juggling a lot of balls in the air at once. In fact, some of you just read this and thought I've repeated the first marketing mistake. Read it again, carefully. It's difficult to make sure every quick quip on social media is spelled correctly, but proofread your posts. A writer saying, "Buy me book!" is like showing up to an interview with your fly open and toilet paper stuck to your shoe. Not a good first impression.

3. All Caps

This one is pretty self-explanatory. All caps is the best way on social media to get ignored or get anger from someone in return. Every time I see a post on my feed in all caps, I feel like Steve Carell's character Brick Tamland from the hit movie *Anchorman*: "I DON'T KNOW WHAT WE'RE YELLING ABOUT!!!!" Keep it mellow and keep your finger off the 'caps lock.'

4. The Solitary Link

If you can't take the time to put thought into your social media post, how can you expect a potential reader to take the time to consider your book? I would love to see the statistics for the success rate of someone randomly clicking on a solitary link with no understanding of what the link is and then deciding to make a purchase when arriving at the linked page. It's got to have the lowest success rate for book sales out there. It's either that or throwing copies of your book out the car window on the highway with a note saying, "Please send a check to..." Instead, include an excerpt of your book or a rave review from a reader. You're bound to find much more success.

5. You Will Love It!

Really? Will I? You don't even know me. Why do you assume I'm going to love it? Don't get me wrong, I appreciate your vigor and passion. I understand the effort you put into creating your book. I commend you for the feat and I wish you all the success in the world. But please don't assume I will love your book. Adamant recommendations from biased authors that do not know me—maybe it works for you, but I just don't see it.

Get creative, people! We all want to sell our work. We all have dreams of success. Find innovative avenues for sales. Don't just figuratively yell at people on social media. The result will be opposite of what you're hoping for.

Question authority.

Indie publishing has blown up the status quo in the publishing industry. Publishing your book has never been easier. Ten years ago, no one would have predicted that Amazon, a bookseller, would be the biggest *book publisher* in the world today. Ten years from now, I guarantee the landscape will be vastly different again. We're amidst more shifting in the industry as publishers and authors try to navigate a world of ever-changing technology.

I mention this because, as a writer, you'll often receive advice from readers, editors, publishers, or a countless number of people, about what you should do to improve your writing. Some of it will be excellent feedback. Some it will be intended to help your writing become better-suited for the market. Ultimately, you need to find your own voice as a writer. Use the advice of others to guide you, but don't feel beholden to write in a style or a genre that will be more marketable.

Don't take the status quo as a requirement. Don't look at how you think everyone else is writing and try to copy it. Find your own voice. Remember what we learned in Tip 7. Find your voice and style, and don't let go of it. Write the REAL YOU.

Don't copy how other authors write. Be your own voice.

Don't take "*their*" word for how you need to publish or what you need to publish. Follow your own path. What do *Harry Potter*, *A Wrinkle in Time*, *Gone with the Wind*, and *Twilight* have in common? They were all initially rejected by publishers, but went on to become massive hits. No one knows what is going to sell and what isn't. Don't let writing a hit be a guide to finding your most authentic path as a writer.

Question authority. Be your own voice.

Question those who question authority.

N ow that we just got done questioning the status quo, let's take a step back. There are people who have been there before. Lean on them. The best way to get to where you want to go is to hang out with people who've been there before. Listen to their advice, it will be invaluable on your writing journey.

Drink in the knowledge of as many authors as you can. Read as much as you can. Take their advice to heart. Inquisitiveness is a gift of the writer.

Drink in the knowledge of as many authors as you can.

The two best ways to become a better writer are to write and to read. Write, write, write! Read, read, read! Don't expect to realize your writing dreams if you're not writing and reading often.

During the marketing tour and efforts for my first fiction book, I was consistently asked by interviewers some variation of the following question: "What piece of advice would you give to aspiring writers?" My answer was always the same.

Over the years, I've been offered an abundance of feedback from mentors and teachers I trust. I have heard excellent commentary from a few creative people who I admire greatly. There are two ideas that have stuck with me throughout all my writing endeavors. These sentiments helped to get me over the hump and—as Brené Brown would say (or Theodore Roosevelt before her)—*Dare Greatly* in my writing endeavors.

1. When asked about the fears and doubts that she had with her writing, Elizabeth Gilbert—best-selling author of *Eat, Pray, Love*—said she finally had an epiphany that her "writing muse" was telling her that this isn't her story. If she doesn't tell it, she bemoaned, then the muse would move on to someone else who will. Ms. Gilbert discussed how freeing this was for her. She was no longer declaring to the reader: "Listen to me. I have something to say." Instead, she was writing through her muse, her inspiration. It was almost as if she had no other choice but to write. This opened her up to write every day without fear of the result.

2. Ira Glass is an American public radio personality and the host and producer of the radio and television show

This American Life. He has a great quote for young creatives. In short, he encourages that your work is not going to be good when you're first starting out. You may have an excitement for your craft and a killer taste for what's good, but your execution is poor. The only way to improve your work, the only way to close the gap so that your work is as good as your ambitions, is to keep writing. Every day. Every week put yourself on a deadline to write something new. It's going to take a while, but that's normal. Good writing doesn't come the first time you sit down.

In short:

1. Don't worry about whether you have anything important to say. If you are inspired, say it.
2. Write often. You won't become a good writer unless you're regularly finding time to write.

Be yourself and be inquisitive. Inquisitiveness is the gift of the writer.

There are countless people before you who have ventured into the writing arena. Lean on them to better hone your craft.

There will come a time when you're presented with decisions that compromise your values, know how you will respond before they happen.

O ne of the most important considerations in reaching any goal in life, is preparation. This is important for us as writers. We need to think about how we'll respond to compromising situations before they happen. The best way to do that is, again, always remember why you started writing in the first place. This needs to be repeated time and again so we don't forget it. If you understand the goals of your writing, then you can anticipate how you will respond to compromising situations.

Let me throw a few examples at you that you're bound to encounter on your writing journey, particularly after you've completed your final manuscript and are putting your work in front of others in the writing community.

1. At some point, you are bound to get feedback on how to make your yet-to-be-published work better. Some of it will be invaluable. Some of it might make you feel like your writing is losing its soul if you follow it. Figure out how you're going to approach editorial and substantive feedback ahead of time. Understand which parts of your writing is the soul and the pulse of the book. Know which passages cannot be cut without losing the creative reason for writing the book. It is equally as important to know when you're trying to be an unnecessary wordsmith and that some of it should be ditched. Thinking about this ahead of time will help you better prepare for the editing process.

2. What are you going to do when someone asks for your book for free? I know, how dare they, right?! Guess what? It's going to happen. And happen. And happen again. People understand that they need to pay for coffee, food, clothes and everything else in life, but when it comes to creative works—music, movies, books, articles, photos, television, audio content—there's a predominant opinion that they should be free. People are going to want your book for free. It helps to remember what your goals are. Are you trying to make a living? Are you trying to reach as many readers as possible? Do you want tons of reviews? If you want as many reviews as possible, or to reach as many readers as you can, then you might decide giving away

your book is the best way to do that. Once you understand why you're writing and what your goals are, draw a line ahead of time on when you will give a book away and when you won't.

3. Once you've completed and published your work, you'll have a difficult time-management decision in front of you. As writers, our creative inclination is to explore what the next book is that's hidden inside us just waiting to be written. As authors, we have countless jobs beyond just writing. We are writers, editors, coders, marketers, writing community supporters, and on and on. If you need to promote your work, decide ahead of time how much marketing you want to do. If you're an organizer, I recommend budgeting your marketing time for the first six months after publication. How much time do you anticipate committing to being an author over the next six months? Break that time into marketing time, social media time, blogging time, author promotion, interview time, and writing time. If not, you'll fall down the rabbit hole of marketing and get overwhelmed or discouraged.

There are countless examples of times in your author-life that you'll be faced with compromising decisions. Know how you'll respond before it happens.

Know how you will respond to compromising situations before they occur.

Remember to get lost in your mind from time to time.

This tip might come naturally for many of you. It is something that writers probably do too much, quite honestly, so it might not necessarily be a reminder we need. As writers, we're always thinking, ruminating, pondering, and then thinking some more. There's a great Eugene Ionesco quote on this point. (For those of you that don't know, Ionesco was a Romanian-French playwright that many acknowledge as the most notable figure in French Avant-garde theatre.)

> **"A writer never has a vacation. For a writer, life consists of either writing or thinking about writing."**
>
> **- Eugene Ionesco."**

This is the case for me, often exhaustingly so. I write down an idea, or a funny scene I encountered, or even more often, _wishing I had remembered_ to write down a moment that later I forgot exactly what it was that struck me at the time. The point is, I'm always thinking about writing. It plagues me so much that when I'm not writing, I feel guilty about it.

This may be the same for you. Writer's don't often have trouble getting lost in their own minds. However, while this seems to be less of a problem during the writing stages, it is more of an issue during the editing, publishing, and marketing stages. We can get too wrapped up in the nitty gritty of marketing and forget to get lost in our thoughts and write.

Don't forget about your writing because you're working hard getting people engaged with your writing. Be selective with how much time you spend on social media or other aspects of the writing community. Certainly, get involved. The last ten tips are clear about that, but don't do it so much that you're writing suffers. Manage your time and stay focused on the craft. What's the point of having a following if you're no longer writing?

Use this as a reminder that first and foremost, you are a writer. Keep writing. Don't be afraid to write about something pointless. Or write about something deeply meaningful to you, but that you know will never see the light of day. Or write gibberish.

Just get lost in your mind today.

Breathe slowly.

T ry it. Seriously, take a moment right now and breath. Breath very slowly. Focus on your breath for a minute. Inhale. Exhale. Slowly and deeply. You'll find yourself more relaxed and focused after that minute.

Go ahead, I'll wait. Let me know when you're back.

Dr. Fred Muench, owner of the company Mobile Health Interventions says, "The main physiological benefit to slower breathing is that it increases oxygen saturation in cells. This unleashes a cascade of positive effects, including giving you more energy and increased cognitive abilities." Which of us as writers wouldn't benefit from more energy and better cognitive focus? I know I would.

Are you stuck on something you're writing about? Breath slowly.

Are you having difficulty finding the time to sit and write? Breathe slowly.

Are struggling to get your book published? Breathe slowly.

Are you completely lost in the marketing process for your book? Breathe slowly.

Remember to breathe. Slowly.

Let me share a real-world example of the benefits of breathing. A little over a year ago, Amazon deleted over 55 reviews on my book *Pieces Like Pottery*. Amazon deletes reviews and always has. They have an obligation to their customers to provide useful and honest product feedback. Individuals are always trying to outsmart Amazon by getting a manufactured boost in positive reviews. The reviews of my book were not that, however. They were honest and genuine.

You can imagine my distress when I learned that all those reviews were deleted. Having credible reader feedback is important for authors. You know what I did before anything else? I stopped and breathed slowly. It reminded me to focus myself and realize that while distressing, it was not catastrophic. It reminded me to recall Tip 23 and Smile. And it allowed me to strategize on how to approach the situation by contacting Amazon representatives on a variety of platforms. If you're wondering, Amazon eventually returned all 55+ deleted reviews. Even if they hadn't, I was in a much better position to accept it by first, breathing.

Remember to breathe. Slowly. Follow your breath and it will lead you to a calm, centered place from which to respond to life's curve balls.

Decide how you define success as a writer.

Success can be forever fleeting, particularly if you base your success on what others think. Success can be a constantly moving target. It can be sand slipping through our fingers. You may go to bed one night feeling like you're achieving greatness and wake up the next morning believing you've totally blown it. Success is a fickle friend.

If your definition is based on whether others enjoy what you do, you're bound to be disappointed. I don't mean whether your wife or your husband or your best friend enjoy what you do, although you may need to include them if you're overly-concerned about what they think. Don't focus on whether the masses enjoy your work. It's easier said than done, but it will be the key to your success and happiness in life.

It's great to have incremental goals in your journey as a writer. Longtime readers of mine know that one of my original goals when I published my first book was to reach 100 sales. It was a modest and simple objective. I'm happy to say that I have sprinted past that finish line. (Thank you to all my wonderful readers and supporters! I'm grateful for you!) Concrete goals like this are healthy. Keep them small, but mighty, and let them grow from there.

Be careful and aware of how you define your success at the end of the day. Your happiness cannot depend on forces outside of your control, otherwise you're bound to become unhappy.

Do what you do and enjoy that you do it, regardless if others do too.

Author, motivational speaker, and financial advisor Suze Orman has a definition of success that I appreciate: "I have decided that when all that you have been defined by ceases to be and you still know who you are and like what you know— then you have truthfully succeeded."

I like this definition of success. It doesn't involve the opinion of others. Too often we base our triumphs on how others receive us, which is not only fleeting, but anxiety-inducing. As authors, we might look at how many books we sell, or how many we write, or how many reviews we get, or how much money we make, but those are all fleeting realities.

Orman's definition of success completely strips the opinion of others from the equation. It leaves you standing there bare and naked, and then asks, "Do you still know and like who you are now that you're standing here bare and naked?"

Adjust how you define success and know that just by finishing and loving even just a page in your book, you have already succeeded.

Have resolve.

We've reached the finish line my friends. Tip 40. Have resolve.

Do you recall from Tip 36 about deciding how to respond to compromising situations before they occur? If you understand why you started writing in the first place—let's call this your internal writing compass—then you can know ahead of time what approach you will take. Once you've figured that out, have resolve to keep writing. Have the strength to stick it out, or as my father would say, have sticktuitiveness. You'll be challenged and tested throughout your journey. Continue showing up to write and giving your all to the craft.

During the editing process for this book, I hit a wall, and a hard one. I was surged with tremendous doubts and fear. I had written nearly the entire book and then struggled to write the final words. In fact, I emailed my editor, "I've been struggling to put together words. I can't stop thinking, 'What do you have to say that's useful anyway? Why would anyone want to get advice from you? This book is nonsense.'"

I used all the tips we've talked about here to get through it. I leaned on my writing community for encouragement and received support from my kind editor (Tips 24 and 25). I wrote nonsense with no purpose for a little bit (Tip 17). I took a step back and adjusted my mindset (Tip 12). I loved myself more and showed myself compassion (Tips 10 and 11). I enjoyed nature (Tip 13), walked barefoot through the grass (Tip 22), enjoyed my friends and family (Tip 14), enjoyed music (Tip 15), and read a book (Tip 19). I stopped to smile (Tip 23), then when I felt sufficiently centered, I grabbed hold of my faith and hope (Tip 21), remembered there is only one me (Tip 6), and latched onto the voice that is the Real You inside of me (Tip 7). Going through all of these steps allowed me to once again, stay conscious of the present (Tip 3) and seize the opportunity in front of me (Tip 1).

These aren't just fluffy, nonsensical tips, friends. They work if you use them and if you have the resolve to keep coming back to write. Don't quit because you've hit speed bumps. Don't quit on what you love! Ever.

"Nothing any good isn't hard."
—F. Scott Fitzgerald

Resolve to keep writing through your doubts and fears, even in the face of negative feedback from readers and critics, and yourself! Don't quit writing because a family member asked what the point of it is. Don't quit because one reviewer said, "Who the hell cares? (yawn.)" If you're worried you might not have the muscle to receive negative criticism about your writing from people, you do. You're stronger than you think and braver than you know.

By the way, that hypothetical review I mentioned—Who the hell cares? (yawn.)— is not hypothetical. That's an actual review of my book *Pieces Like Pottery*. Dozens and dozens of five star reviews, and that is an actual review of someone who bought my book. That's great! That was her impression and I'm glad she shared it. If my books don't have lovers and haters, then I failed to dare creatively.

You can handle reviews like that. You can handle the criticism, the long nights, the pain, the rejection. Trust me, you can! You started writing for a reason. See it through! Don't give up at the first sign of adversity. Or the second. Or the third. Or the hundredth sign.

You started writing for a reason. See it through!

Expect dragons.

A bonus tip free of charge. Tip 41. You're welcome. When I started writing, I did a lot of blogging and some paid writing for various legal and financial firms. I always tried to hone my voice as a fiction writer, but all of my public written works were non-fiction. In private, I wrote and wrote and wrote. I worked on *Pieces Like Pottery* for seven years. Finally, with the encouragement of my lovely wife, I decided it was time let it go and offer it to the public.

Knowing nothing about publishing a book, I read everything I could to learn how to navigate my way. I started by contacting well over 100 literary magazines and agents. My hope was that an agent would love my book and help me get published. I also hoped a magazine would pick up a story of mine and it would give me a stamp of credibility when speaking with agents.

Guess what? No one wanted it. I didn't even get a nibble. Not one of them were interested enough to consider publishing a story or representing my book. In fact, most of the responses were form letters, (or more accurately form emails). It didn't go well. After over 100 rejections, I was left with two options. One, quit and go home. Two, self-publish.

> **There will come a point in your writing life when you'll be faced with the option to quit.**
>
> **If you love it, don't quit. Keep writing, even if it's just for yourself.**

I chose the self-publishing route and am grateful I did. It has been a long and arduous road, and I'm sure it will continue to be so for quite a while, but I wouldn't change it for anything. I've learned and gained more than I could have imagined. I've connected with some amazing authors. Most importantly, I've found the confidence to move forward on this writing journey again and again.

I'm not trying to give you a history of my first years as a published fiction author. I'm also not trying to tell you what will work or not work for you. What *I am* trying to say is to expect anything as a writer. Expect Dragons.

The road to publication may look daunting, but it's supposed to look that way. Don't view that as an impediment, view it as an opportunity to learn, to gain insight, and to reach goals small and large. Most importantly, use it as an opportunity to discover who you are as a writer.

You have tremendous resources all around you. Use them! Publishing is more readily available than ever before in the history of man. Break your goal of getting published (or getting published again) down into small attainable steps, then check them off one by one.

You can't do it all at once, so don't try. And you certainly don't know what's going to happen, so expect those dragons. Be prepared for rejection, it will happen! Just as importantly, be prepared for success!

A lot of people are afraid to fail, but they don't recognize that they are just as afraid to succeed. Prepare for your success! If you don't, there's only one dragon you need to look out for, because failure will be coming.

Let me know how I can help you on your journey. If I can, I will. Know that you have every resource available to you to reach your goals. Most importantly, right inside of you is a well to draw from and fill up as you need. You *can* finish your book. You *can* get published. You *can* sell hundreds of copies, and you *can* become a bestseller. And most likely, you will do that process all over again. Keep the faith, keep writing and keep doing it for the love of it.

Good luck my friends! Come back early and come back often.

NOTES FOR AUTHORS

NOTES FOR AUTHORS

NOTES FOR AUTHORS

NOTES FOR AUTHORS

Acknowledgements

I have been blessed with wonderful family and wonderful friends in the writing community. Thank you all for your love, support, and encouragement. I would be remiss if I did not acknowledge a number of individuals specifically.

Jon Balsbaugh: Once again, your "101 College Tips" inspired the concept used in Expect Dragons, which in turn inspired the formation of this book. Thank you for always inspiring our class years ago.

Kimberly Coleman: Thank you for encouragement and inspiration. If it weren't for your insistence, this book would have never been written. Thank you!

Assaph Mehr: I'm grateful for your support and guidance as we wander on this writing journey 12,000 miles apart.

Leslie Caplan: Your editing suggestions were wonderful. You were instrumental in reordering and restructuring this book. It would have never become what it is if you weren't there beside me as my editor.

To my parents: Thank you for instilling a love of reading in my soul.

William: You make me laugh every single day. Thank you for bringing so much joy to my life.

Isla: Continue to be the amazing, curious young woman that you are. I love each and every adventure with you.

Sara: I could never say it enough. Thank you for supporting and loving this wayward writer. I'm grateful to have a best friend like you. You are more than a man could ask for. I'm lucky to have you by my side.

ABOUT THE AUTHOR

Dan Buri is a trusted resource for writers to gain insight into the difficult world of indie publishing. His first collection of short fiction—Pieces Like Pottery—which has been recognized on multiple Best Seller Lists, is an exploration of heartbreak and redemption. His nonfiction works have been distributed online and in print, in publications including Pundit Press, Tree, Summit Avenue Review, American Discovery, and TC Huddle.

Dan is a founding member of the Independent Writers Guild, a worldwide organization of writers and publishing professionals dedicated to promoting the interest of indie writers by encouraging public interest in, and fostering an appreciation of, quality indie literature. He is an active attorney in the Pacific Northwest. He lives in Oregon with his wife and two young children.

ALSO BY DAN BURI

<u>AMAZON #1 BESTSELLER</u>. The first collection of short fiction from Dan Buri, *Pieces Like Pottery*, announces the arrival of a new American author. Critics are raving:

"*Pieces Like Pottery* hits you in the feels." - *CJ Leger, The San Francisco Globe*

"Immensely powerful, challenging, and emotionally-charged. 5 Stars." -*Stacey Garrity, Whispering Stories*

"Something to be cherished and relived. 5 Stars." -*Devi Nair, The Verdicts Out*

"We can all learn from this book. 5 Stars." -*Colleen Ozment, Paws and Paper*

"Wow. Read this book. 5 Stars." -*Megan Verwey, GirlPlusBook*

In this distinct selection of stories marked by struggle and compassion, *Pieces Like Pottery* is a powerful examination of the sorrows of life, the strength of character, the steadfast of courage, and the resiliency of love requisite to find redemption.

Filled with graceful insight into the human condition, each linked story presents a tale of loss and love mirroring themes from each of the five Sorrowful Mysteries. A collection of nine stories, each exquisitely written and charged with merciful insight into the trials of life, Pieces Like Pottery reminds us of the sorrows we all encounter in life and the kindness we receive, oftentimes from the unlikeliest of places.

BUY *PIECES LIKE POTTERY* NOW

Printed in Great Britain
by Amazon